Positioning You To Meet The Mark

Prophetic Guide 101:

Your Guide For Simplistic and Resourceful Teachings

Volume 2

Ashley Reynolds

Prophetic Guide 101: Your Guide for Simplistic and Resourceful Teachings

By: Ashley Reynolds

Book Cover: Jasmine Miller

Published by J. Elaine Writes

www.jelainewrites.com

This document is published by J. Elaine Writes located in the United States of America. It is protected by the United States Copyright Act, all applicable state laws and international copyright laws.

Printed in the United States of America

ISBN: 978-1-7332352-4-2

Abstract:

You are not alone. You have Help.

There is a difference between being a prophesier and a prophet. I want you to know that according to Deuteronomy 18:15-22 (especially 21-22), that you are not a prophet because you prophesy. You might be thinking, well this scripture looks like prophets were chosen by the accuracy of their prophesying. Well, let's look at this text through a careful lens. This scripture is teaching us how that the accuracy of the prophet's word caused men to know that he was indeed a prophet from the Lord. Notice how that the prophet's ability to be known by the people as being a prophet was due to his word manifestation, but not as the source to which would validate as being the thing that chose him to be a prophet. So, the prophecy manifestation was for the people's sake while the choosing of the prophet belonged to the Lord. Let's look at what God would do in the midst of a people in Deuteronomy 18:15, "The Lord your God will raise up for you a prophet like me from among your own brothers. You must listen to him." (NIV) Once again I say, "You are a prophet not because you prophesy, but because God said that that is who you are." I hear you asking the question, well don't prophesiers who are not called to the office of a prophet prophesy too? How can we tell who is the prophesier and who is the prophet? I'm glad you are curious to learn. We will go into that later in this book and in the manual.

Many have self-ordained themselves or have allowed others to pump them up into becoming a prophet. This happens only because they speak words of knowledge, wisdom or prophecy occasionally. People are being coerced into thinking that they are prophets not on account of God's choice but on account of fleshly opinion. This is dangerous. The Scripture in 1 Corinthians 14:5 expresses the heart's desire of the authority figure in the person of the Apostle Paul. Paul expresses his wish that all of God's people would prophesy. We can see throughout both the old and new testament how the Prophets and Apostles were given the ability to pray that others prophesy. However, let's look at an authority that one prophet wished for but did not have the authority to bring into fruition. Read Numbers 11:26- 29, was right after God and Moses partnered together to select and anoint those who would help Moses with handling those he led. Moses and God were both frustrated due to the people's complaints and indignant behavior. Medad and Eldad were registered among the people but were not chosen to be one of the 70 that should go outside of the camp to receive the spirit of God and the ability to prophesy. Medad and Eldad begin to prophesy. This brought on controversy with some. A young boy had a problem with it as well as Moses' adjutant, Joshua. They wanted Moses to stop Medad and Eldad from prophesying. This was probably because of three things:

☐ Moses was absent from those left behind inside of the camp and it was improper to act as a prophet or to even prophesy in the absence of the leader of the camp.

☐ Medad and Eldad were not chosen to be a part of the 70 and to receive the spirit

☐ Maybe Joshua felt a little threatened that this could impede him from being Moses successor.

Nonetheless, Moses was in the beginning stage of having some relief with having to deal with God's obstinate people. Moses probably had not been able to really enjoy having some relief from the weight of carrying the people and was probably still a little bothered in his spirit by all that had been going on. When Moses answered Joshua, he spoke a desire of his heart but not of God's will. He stated that he wished that all of Israel would become prophets. This was in defense of Medad and Eldad but not the will of God. Moses in this moment overstepped his boundary as a prophet of God to pray or decree something that only God had the power to determine. Listen to the revelation behind both 1 Corinthians 14:5 and Numbers 11:29 in that it points to the truth that while apostles and prophets can pray that the people of God prophesy, they do not have the authority or power to choose who would be a prophet. Only God can choose.

Ephesians 4:11, proves that though man may desire all to walk in this prophetic office, only some have been chosen and anointed by God to take on the task. What prophesying makes you is a vessel that the Lord is using to prophetically speak forth His word in the earth. The prophet has his/her place as well as the prophesier. Whether a prophesier or a prophet there is room for all in the Lords kingdom. Be sure of your place. Let God reveal to you who you are. Whatever God reveals to you in the dark, he will confirm in the light. God will confirm it through your mentor, another prophet of the Lord, or your pastor. Make your callings and elections sure. We will discuss this later in the book / manual.

You Are Not Alone

I want you to know that most prophets wrestle with self-esteem issues. They deal with identity dysfunction. Many of them deal heavily with the spirit of sexual perversion. Though this perversion is demonically influenced, I believe that the foundation that it thrives off of is the prophets lack of true self identity. When you know who you are in Christ Jesus, you have a greater propensity to fulfill Ephesians 6:13. Depression is another area of warfare that prophets deal with. We will discuss this later in this book. If you are reading this and you feel as though you are alone with dealing with these issues, please go talk with your pastor, mentor, youth leader or someone with whom you feel is biblically sound and who have your best interest at heart. You are not alone. You have help young prophet.

Forward

"I remember sitting in a church service years ago experiencing the prophetic ministry of Ashley Reynolds. She was on a program to render a selection but when given the microphone she made a prophetic declaration. The Lord gave her 2 words and those 2 words turned into a complete song that shifted that atmosphere. I was blown away by the uniqueness of her call. Many are called but few are chosen and it was in that moment I knew Ashley Reynolds was anointed, appointed, and chosen by God for such a time as this. From that day to this day I have watched God take Ashley deeper & deeper in him, rightly dividing his word while helping others get clarity, revelation, and in all things getting understanding. As a young prophet, she has experienced what she is now using to help other young prophets along their journey. Teaching the difference between a prophet and a prophesier is vital in this era especially with so many self ordained individuals in the body. Ashley Reynolds lives a life that proves she is a 20th century Prophet equipped and qualified by God. Prophetic Simplistic Guide 101 was inspired and written by the Holy Ghost through Ashley to help true sons & daughters that have been chosen in this hour as a mouthpiece for God. This Prophetic Simplistic Guide 101, will help many young prophets embrace their call and rise above the stereotypes that has kept them from maturing and walking in the full potential of their office. The word of God is a lamp unto your feet, a light unto your path, and there is nothing more educational than a true experience from God to help you along the way."

Pastor Salena Eason

CEO/Founder Changing Seasons Ministry Savannah Georgia

www.changingseasonsministry.org

Prophetic Guide 2: Table of Contents:

Part 20: Logos and Rhema Word

There are two dimensions of prophecy. The logos word and the rhema word. The word of God is and has always been the strongest reference point for the prophets. It is the word of God or the scroll, which undergirds the prophet's ministry, making it relevant for the readers. As seen in the life of King Hezekiah, there are some prophecies (futuristic happenings) that can be changed while other prophetic utterances will not be changed. The 2 kinds of prophetic words that can go forth are:

1. The logos word- referred to as the written word; does not change; stands forever
2. The rhema word- can change; this is a more revelatory word which extends from the logos word

Let's examine them both. The logos word can be defined as the written word. It is referred to as being the 66 books of the bible. The logos word was written by holy, inspired men. It is viewed as being prophetic books which houses the wisdom and counsel of God. It is through these written prophecies that men can rest their conscience and be assured that as surely as the Lord had spoken it, it shall come to pass. The logos word can be used as weaponry to combat the present demons that arise to taunt our future promises. Let's examine some scriptures, which can never be changed

1. 1 Timothy 1:18- this Apostle Paul, reminds Timothy of the unchangeable word which was written in the lineage of his ancestors and that still stands as a promise and means of war for him presently.

2. Hebrews 7:15-18- This written prophetic logos was set in stone as a promise to king David that his kingdom should be everlasting and that out of his dynasty should arise a priest which should reign forever.

3. In both Luke 4 and Matthew 4 accounts we see Jesus leaning upon the logos to defeat the devil that had arisen to challenge him, his identity and his authority as the son of God. Jesus was smart enough to depend upon the logos to fight the devil.

It is the logos (written word) that prophesiers and prophets can use to prophetically discern the seasons. The logos word serves as a counseling tool to which the prophet can turn to receive confirmation on the prophetic words that they receive from the Lord. In my opinion, it is the logos word which serves as the safest prophetic utterance that prophets release. It is a sure word that will never change. Jesus declared that heaven and earth might fade away, but not one jot or tittle of his word would fade. The Apostle Paul records in 1 Corinthians 13:8, that prophecies will fail. This is not to say that God is incapable of bringing his word to pass, but simply that he may change his mind.

This brings me to the rhema word (revelatory word; changeable word) which can be referred to as a fresh word. The rhema is the extension of the logos word. With the written word (logos) there is hidden manna which can only be seen with your spiritual eye. The rhema word is the revelation of the written word. It is released in correspondence to the word of God. When it is released it is usually an in-season word which matches your present-day situation. However, this rhema word can change as you evolve in the word of the Lord or simply at the will of the father. This means that you can read the logos (written) word today and receive an understanding of that word. God can give you a rhema word off of that scripture as it concerns your "now" season. However, you can go back and read the same logos word 5 years later and the revelation on that scripture would have changed on account of the fact that you have evolved in your life experience. Let's examine some scriptures on the rhema word: (READ)

1. 1 Samuel 10:6- "And the Spirit of the Lord will come upon thee, and thou shalt prophesy with them, and shalt be turned into another man." It was in this moment that the spirit of the Lord had come upon Samuel to prophesy a rhema word unto Saul in that moment. It spoke of what God would do in Saul's life.

2. Judges 3:10- "The Spirit of the Lord came on him, and he judged Israel. Othniel went out to battle, and the Lord handed over Cushan-rishathaim king of Aram to him, so that Othniel overpowered him." It was in this moment that the spirit of the Lord had come on

Othniel to release a revelation that he would gain victory. We see how Othniel wins in the end.

3. Numbers 11:25- "Then the Lord descended in the cloud and spoke to him. He took some of the Spirit that was on Moses and placed the Spirit on the 70 elders. As the Spirit rested on them, they prophesied, but they never did it again." In this scripture we can see how when the spirit of the Lord had come upon them how that they would prophesy a rhema word in that moment. However, it only lasted a season.

The rhema word (prophecy) as well as the logos word, which is also prophecy has the power to edify, exhort and comfort those that would listen. (Read 1 Corinthians 14:3) I encourage you to stick with the word while asking God to give you his rhema (right now) word.

Part 21: The Spirit of Paranoia

In this section we will discuss how paranoia enters a prophet's life in order to make them believe the lies that are presented to their mind. With this spirit of paranoia comes the struggle of trust and loyalty.

When someone becomes paranoid, it is because of the "spirit" behind the activity that is antagonizing their soul and mind. It is mental derangement, which comes to disturb the peace in the prophet's life. The greatest battle for the prophet happens in his mind. The attack of this spirit of paranoia is to bring the thought pattern under subjection and into the captivity of fear. The motive of this is to cause the prophet to become out of range with the prophetic assignment on his or her life. It's all about the hindrance of the prophet's movement in that he will become immobilized in the progression of his destiny. This spirit comes to cause the prophet's mind to come to a standstill due to his thoughts being taken hostage.

Let's examine the life of the prophet Elijah and how this spirit of paranoia tried to antagonize the prophet's life found in 1Kings 19:1-18: You must read this verse to better understand these points.

☐ vs 1- The prophet had just got finished doing a good work by killing off all of Jezebel's false prophets. In this was the Lord pleased

☐ vs 2- It's normally after you have accomplished a work for God by tearing down demonic works that the enemy will send attacks to you out of retaliation.

☐ vs 3- unfortunately the prophet became overwhelmed by fear that this demonic message from jezebel would be as it was written for his life. (It even caused him to abandon his servants)

☐ vs 4- this spirit of paranoia had driven the prophet into desiring to die. This is another tactic of this spirit which is to provoke you into premature death. It wants to cause you to self-sabotage your own life and destiny.

☐ vs 5-8- Elijah became weakened after his victory by killing off the false prophets. When he got a message of doom from Jezebel, he became terrorized by a spirit of paranoia. However, in verses 5-8, we see how that the prophet was comforted by the angel of the Lord through the instructions to eat, drink, and to go to the mountain of God.

☐ vs 9-10- However, it is possible to arrive to the place where God dwells and still be bothered by paranoia.

☐ vs 11-18- God visits the prophet. The only way for the prophet to get delivered from this spirit of paranoia is that he has an encounter with God.

Saul was not a prophet but he was a king whom the Lord did allow to join in with the company of prophets to prophesy at times. So, this simply means that he was a prophesier. Let's examine how the spirit of paranoia impacted his life sorely:

☐ 1 Samuel 16:14- When the spirit of the Lord departed from Saul there was a release of a distressing spirit that troubled Saul from the Lord. It sounds like paranoia.

☐ 1 Samuel 28: 4-7- out of desperation did Saul seek after a medium. The spirit behind his desperation was paranoia. He was paranoid at the fact that he saw this philistine army coming towards him and because God would not comfort him about it, he became paranoid at what would happen to him.

Young prophet whenever you become overwhelmed with a spirit or paranoia begin to call on the name of Jesus. He can help. However, if you're on medication for this, take your medicine and keep calling on Jesus. He will answer prayer.

Part 22: The Prophet and Offense

The importance of releasing daily offenses and hurts is a vital part in order that the prophet remains spiritually healthy. In this section we will discuss how important it is for the prophet of God to release daily offenses in order to keep their spirits free from clogs of the spirit.

The spirit of offense is a direct attack against one's growth in Christ. The definition of Offense means to commit a crime or wrongdoing against someone or law. One other spirit that usually accompanies this spirit of offense is the spirit of unforgiveness. When offense and unforgiveness settles in a person's heart, they become stifled in their personal development. I am here to warn you that for as long as you live you will have the opportunity to be offended. Offense will meet you daily. However, it is what you do with the offense that will matter the most. You need to know that to be or not to be offended is your choice.

Let's examine some signs that people express when they are offended by you:

1. They will withdraw from you

2. They will shut down while in conversation with you

3. Their attitude will change towards you

4. They will verbally tell you that they are offended

Part of the definition of offense is to commit a misdemeanor or a felon. The revelation that I get out of these is that offense can escalade from a misdemeanor to a felony.

Misdemeanor offenses are small offenses. The price you pay for committing them is not as great, yet they can still cause some level of damage. Spiritually speaking they can start off with someone walking by without speaking unintentionally, not offering help to someone in need, saying something that you did not think would be offensive (miscommunication), not inviting someone out to your gatherings etc... These can all graduate into becoming a felony offense if ignored or not dealt with.

"Discern the people around you" and "discern your relationships." You have to do what the Apostle Paul said, "to labor to know the spirit of those you are amongst. This will help you to know how best to care for them.

Offenses escalate into the felony level because people are not willing to admit that they were offended at the small things. We are afraid of being judged by others because what admitting to offenses does is expose our vulnerabilities. Prophets deal with this the heaviest. While all ministry gifts deal with it, I believe that prophets deal with this the strongest. Pride steps in because we want others to believe that "nothing bothers us or gets under our skin." This is only because many of us don't want to be seen as being weak. Confessing our offenses puts us at an advantage because the devil won't have any grounds or legal holds on us to hinder our spiritual growth.

Examples of felony offenses are as such:

1. Deliberately trying to make others jealous/envious of you

2. Lying on the character of another

3. Malicious acts (trying to hinder one's progress)

4. Gossip

How to handle offenses through scripture: (Read)

1. Mark 6:1-4- Jesus had a revelation that people of his past would have a hard time receiving him. He did not fight them. Jesus simply shook the dust off of his feet and moved on to another town. Don't fight people; just move forward.

2. 1 Corinthians 8:9- wisdom speaks and instructs that when others are offended by you, stop such behavior around them. Offense will then be defeated.

3. 2 Corinthians 6:3 - live in such a way until the spirit of offense will have no excuse to live among you

4. Proverbs 18:19 - wait until the offended one has cooled down before trying to prove your innocence

5. Matthew 11:6 - don't live reckless

Part 23: The Person Outside of the Prophetic

In this section we will discuss how God is as concerned about your personal life just as much as he is concerned about the prophetic side of who you are. We will see how that God is in love with the person and not their prophetic mantle or gift of prophecy, though both have their place. According to 3John 2, God is concerned about the prophet's holistic well-being.

Do you know who you are?

There is one question that should be at the top of your self-assessment list and that is: "Do I know who I am?" Did you know that it is possible to be strong prophetically but weak and insecure as a person? I believe that this happens because when you prophesy it is not in your own might, strength or spirit that you are functioning, but that of the Lord's strength. Yes, you are taken over in that moment by the spirit of God and made strong to speak forth the Lord's proverbial, apocalyptic or poetic mysteries. Having the correct self-identity is supreme while operating in the prophetic office or the prophetic ministry. We will examine why the prophet needs identity security and how having the right perspective of the self can help the prophet in their flow of the prophetic. We will examine how prophets must come to the realization that after regeneration they are spiritual beings having a natural experience. The prophetic in any sense is totally predicated upon one's spiritual walk so much so that the prophet will need to live by the spirit in order to activate it. If this is not understood, then the prophet will operate from a fleshly standpoint and will miss the true depth of his or her prophetic assignment in the earth. This is to say that whenever God deals with the prophet; though he might use a natural "thing" to draw his or her attention, the full prophetic message will only be caught when he or she decides to elevate in the spirit.

Oftentimes when you ask a person what their identity is, there is usually about a 2-minute delay in answer. I often thought that this delay was a direct exposure on how people lack spending the necessary time, effort and energy to know themselves. We are more alike than we are different, and I feel as though many of us would rather spend more time knowing about others than having to face who we really are. We fail to realize that it is after we know and accept ourselves that we will have healthy and satisfying relationships. It is impossible to authentically accept in others what we will not first accept in ourselves. When we accept ourselves, it makes it easier for us to grant the freedom for others to be their true selves around us. We will offer a no-judgment zone. Through having conversations with many, I found out that many people do not know who they are due to lack of intimacy (into me see) with the self. Instead of spending time with ourselves, it's as if we find greater pleasure by sitting with people who are limited of revelation about us to tell us about who we are. I see this as a person trying to have self-identity insurance. Just in case someone told us something that we didn't like, we could blame them and not ourselves as to the reason why we couldn't grow and be better. (think about this) Most times when people are asked who they are they mostly answer with verbs:

☐ I feed sheep

☐ I build businesses

☐ I write books

☐ I sing songs

☐ I treat patients at a hospital

☐ I am a typist

☐ I teach history

☐ I prophesy.... I evangelize.... I preach..etc....

While all of these verbs describe what you do, they do not describe who you are as a person. You are not what you do. You are who you be. Selah!!!! Verbs point to your functional duties but who you are is underneath it. I believe we exalt our "verbs", or what we do, to people because we have a natural instinct to shine light on our accomplished selves with high hopes that we would be accepted by them. Please understand young prophet that it is natural to want to have a sense of belonging. We were made to be interdependent, not independent. However, I want to take this time to empower you to know that if people are only drawn to you because of your function and not for appreciation of who you are, then you are about to become tied to bondage. This will mean that the only way to keep these people a part of your life will be for you to keep doing and not simply being. As soon as you stop doing this for these types of people, you will often see how that the connection between you and them was never founded upon your true self but only the part of you used for service.

For example, if Peter was new to an athletic organization and all of a sudden he was not capable of performing at the level that they hired him to perform, Peter would surely be fired. While they are firing Peter's function, they cannot fire Peter as a person. This is because Peter (the person) showed up with an ability (function). Before Peter or the team ever discovered his athletic abilities, Peter was still a person. When they fire Peter, it is not his person that they are firing but rather his athletic abilities. While people may deny your function they do not have the power to deny who you are as a person. Young prophet you should never allow the sudden in- capabilities of your talent or gift diminish who you are as a person. You should never allow the termination of a job or the rejection of people cause you to have feelings of dejection about who you are as a person. The value is not in your gift alone. The value is in you. This means that though you may be let go from the team because of unforeseen circumstances, knowing who you are and that the value is in you will allow for you to bounce back with energy to create again.

Now, I want to clarify that there are people who are to be benefitted by your function as being a prophet. Please understand me, there is a place for your function. Young prophet God gave you this function to prophesy and to help with the promotion of His kingdom. I want to tell you that God has a people that will walk with you despite you prophesying or not. These people are anointed by God to accept and engage with the personal side of who you are, and it will have nothing to do with your functions. You will also be called to befriend people for who they are and not for what they do as well. This will be a divine connection and place of reprieve for the both of you.

Part 24: The Prophet and Emotionalism

Prophets are attacked the heaviest in their emotions and in their minds. However, this section is dedicated to discussing the prophet and the emotional battles that they endure. We will discuss why these emotional attacks come, what the prophet should do while going through these emotional crises and what to do after the emotional crisis has ended.

What are emotions and how does it work for us

Emotions can be defined as a natural instinctive state of mind deriving from one's circumstances, mood, or relationships with others. The bible teaches that even Jesus released an emotion when he got news of his friends' death (John 11:35 Jesus wept). We can also see in the story of Joseph how he wept when in the presence of his brethren (Genesis 45:1 (NIV)). We can examine the lives of Mary and the other women when they wept at the death of Jesus Christ. We can see through scripture how that emotions are good for helping us to identify, embrace and release the correct emotion for the circumstances at hand. A person with healthy emotions is one that is in touch with the momentary truth of their life and honest about how it makes them feel. They are open to express freely on how certain events truly affect their emotions. However, some people are taught not to release certain emotions as it would cause for others to view them in a more negative than positive light. In light of this degrading viewpoint, they are taught to abandon their true self in order that others may be appeased with who they are. I believe that the mandatory efforts instilled by governors for people to wear masks due to COVID-19, is a prophetic imagery. People covering their faces with cloth can represent a means for one to conceal their true identity. For image sake, these people hold in how they really feel about their life events and thus are headed for tragedy. For the prophet, this is a sure way to have a head on collision

I would like to inform you that most budding prophets are unhappy while going through early prophetic maturation. This is the stage whereby many of them have a hard time managing their emotional imbalances all because they do not know what is going on with them spiritually. Notice the significance in the definition of emotions in that they can derive from the person or from others. This is where most of the frustration with the prophet's emotions dwell, in that they cannot discern if the emotional disturbance is coming from within or without. Prophets are feelers. This means that not only do they have to face their own inner emotions, but they can also easily pick up on the emotional state of those around them. This can be benefiting as well as harmful to the prophet. It can be benefitting, because the prophet will be able to pray and intercede on behalf of the people with whom they are carrying in their spirit. However, it can be harmful to the prophet if he or she does not learn to cast it upon the Lord. The prophet feels the burden of others and is called to pray for them. After the prophet prays, they should release it out of their spirit. Carrying the weight of others can become overwhelming for the prophet and if not careful he or she could potentially slip into some sort of depression. Cast all of your cares upon God, for He cares for you.

Why does the enemy attack the emotional well-being of the prophet?

In times when your creative abilities are not active you may testify that it is during these times that you experience less warfare, if any at all. However, it is during times when you have received a kingdom assignment from the Lord that you start experiencing the darts against your emotional well-being. The emotions are closely in alignment with the soulish part of you. It is out of this soul part of you that you operate. Everything that you do is connected to what's going on in your soul. In Genesis 2:7, it reads how that God breathed into man's nostrils and that the soul became alive. God created you with great intent. Everything that God created you to accomplish in this life has a time period. When God awakens your prophetic senses to do a work the devil sends a demonic attack on your emotions to suppress you from the "joy" and the "peace" of fulfilling it. Let's examine some symptoms on how you can identify that you are under an emotional attack from hell:

- You feel sluggish in your thoughts and in your movements
- You become overly sensitive about things that would not normally bother you
- You cry more during this time. Your tears are without any true purpose

- You find it difficult to understand the significance of doing your prophetic God assignment

- You see everything through dead lens- There is no life in your vision

- It's hard for you to get excited

- You are mean spirited when you are normally nice

What should the Prophet do while under attack?

When under great emotional affliction pray and reach out to those who are strong. The bible teaches that the strong should uplift and carry the weak. Do not deny how you really feel. When asked what is going on with your emotions, BE HONEST. I can not tell you how annoying it is when someone avails themselves to helping somebody and they are not honest. Honest people recieve the help that they need. Fake people remain sick because they are not honest. Be honest young prophet. It's ok to not be ok sometimes. It's not the end for you.

What should the Prophet do when the emotional attack has lifted?

When you have been freed from emotional bondage do three things:

- Thank God for your freedom

- Appreciate the one who was there praying with you through your emotional frenzy

- Keep the truth before you. This will help to combat the lies that the devil will bring once you are free

Part 25: The Prophet and Obedience

The whole ministry of the prophet is based upon obedience and faith. We have already discussed faith and its role in the ministry of the prophet (See the faith section). Obedience is one's total compliance towards God. The prophet may hear or have in depth prophetic visual perception but will not be able to grow into his or her full potential if he or she does not obey what God has asked them to do. In this section we will examine some of how obedience towards God can be to the prophet's advantage as well as how disobedience to what the Lord requires of him or her can be to the prophet's disadvantage. We will examine how it is life changing that the prophet should obey God whether than man.

What is obedience? We need to first establish that obedience to God is not bondage. Being obedient towards God is not a way for God to hold you captive to his good, perfect and pleasing will. It is not a means of manipulation of any kind. Obedience is a choice. It's your choice. Although God would desire for you to obey his will for your life, he is not desperate. Everything that he has predestined for you to do and you choose not to do it can still be done, but through someone else. If you won't do it, God will raise someone else up to get the job done. Obedience is your invitation from the Lord to soar into your greatest potential. This is to ensure that you may have the opportunity to live and thrive in your prophetic destiny.

Most importantly your obedience is bigger than you. When the Lord brought forth a prophet, He did so because He has always had a people in mind to reach. Most times a prophet is raised up and sent out for the deliverance of a nation of people who are enslaved to the demonic systems and strongholds of this Babylonian cosmos. Let's examine 1 Samuel 16:4, "So Samuel did what the Lord said, and went to Bethlehem. And the Elders of the town trembled at his coming, and said, "do you come peaceably?" Prophets carried such an authoritative spirit and was revered in those days that at their sight would the people tremble. I pray that your prophetic ministry will be filled with such the presence of the Lord that men will begin to reassess their lives out of fear of the God that you carry. Remember it's not you that men will fear but the God that you carry in your prophetic vessel. Your prophetic obedience to the instruction of the Lord elevates you in the authority of God to establish kings in the earth after his heavenly establishment. In verse 3 of 1 Samuel, we see how a prophetic ability was given to the prophet Samuel in that He would be able to anoint a king into office.

Who should the prophets obey? God or man? This section might be a tough read because of what I am going to suggest later. However, I want to start with the Scripture where the Apostles said, "We would rather obey God than man." (Acts 5:29) It has always been taught to me that all participants in the kingdom of God should obey God. Obeying God should be at the top of every believer's agenda. Obedience is not only for the lay members (those without titles) to practice, but also for the Apostle, Prophet, Evangelist,

Pastor, Teacher and leader. Everybody should obey God. The prophet is the messenger of the Lord. This means that he or she receives instructions and direction from the Lord for a person or for a whole church. The prophet of the Lord should never take on the spirit which believes that the prophetic words spoken to the church applies to everyone except them. This leads to a prideful and haughty spirit. One of the greatest truths and secret successes of the prophet's ministry is that he or she obeys the prophetic word first. That's right! They reflect the prophetic word.

I would like to make mention that there is a time and a place where we should obey the voice of our leaders. Let's examine Romans 13:1-3, it teaches us how that we cannot possibly be in full obedience towards God when we are in direct disobedience to His chosen authoritative figures. Now, with saying this I want to clarify that we are only commanded to obey men whom God has put in authority over us when it complies with his word.

Let me also clarify that you do not have to feel guilty by not wanting to go along with something that your authority figure, be it spiritual or political, has commanded you to do because it defies the word of the Lord. There is a respectful way to ask to be dismissed from following through with such instructions.

I also want to clarify that as a prophet you will have many opportunities to disagree with a word of instruction from your leader that is not necessarily wrong or erroneous doctrine. This is different from the situation when something is asked of you that is not in alignment with God's word. Let's examine two obedience concerns:

☐ An accurate word that you do not agree with- as a prophet you must be careful not to decline following through with an instruction given by your Pastor on the basis that you do not agree. You must NOT allow your feelings to get in the way of obedience to God's word. Though you may not agree with your Pastor or with political leaders, it does not mean that it is inaccurate information. Understand that normally, that feeling of disagreement will fade away. Obey now, even when you disagree. Later you will look up and be appreciative of your obedience. Your obedience is your key to greater.

☐ Instructions that are contrary to the Word of God- We are only commanded to obey the instructions of the Lord. However, we must watch the attitude as well as the approach that we take when we have decided not to obey erroneous doctrine or instructions. We must still reverence the position of these leaders though we disagree with their content.

Why should we obey? Isaiah 1:19, (living bible) "If you will only let me help you, if you will only obey, then I will make you rich!" Young prophet obeying God will set you up to access the riches of the spirit and of the natural. Your willing spirit will cause you to reap the bountiful blessings that are closed off from the disobedient. The harvest of souls will be yours. The riches of his secrets will be yours. Your obedience to God will cause you to walk in doors that were shut. Obedience towards God will cause you to have a job that you do not qualify for. It will get you discounts on your dream home. You will drive brand new cars for a discounted price. Young prophet most of all it will cause you to have a rich and valued relationship with God. Obey God!

The Prophet and disobedience- Isaiah 1:20 (living bible) "But if you keep on turning your backs and refusing to listen to me, you will be killed by your enemies; I the lord have spoken." Wrapped up in your obedience towards God is life. It is when we refuse or disobey God's instruction, we enter a danger zone of being defeated by our enemies. Deuteronomy 28:15-19 is another example of what can happen to anyone including the prophet if he or she does not obey. Curses are released upon one's life. Let's examine the Scripture:

" If you won't listen to the Lord your God and won't obey these laws, I am giving you today, then all of these curses shall come upon you:

- Curses in the city

- Curses in the fields

- Curses on your fruit and bread

- The curse of barren wombs

- Curses upon your crops

- Curses upon the fertility of your cattle and flocks

- Curses when you come in

- Curses when you go out

Young prophet you must make up in your mind to obey God because this applies to you too. You are not exempt.

Part 26: The Prophet and Warfare

The prophet and his prophetic mantle are of great value to the body of Christ. It was God, creator of heaven and earth that thought that the establishment of the prophet was necessary. One of the major blessings that prophets add to the body of Christ is the ability to become one step ahead of the devil's agenda. Prophets are an advantage to the body of Christ. They are on the same schedule with God. Amos 3:7, reveals how rich the relationship is between God and his prophets. What an honor it is to be seen as a necessity by God and how he partners with his prophets before making any moves or decisions. With saying this, it is according to Amos 3:3 that the prophet must agree with what God reveals to him or her. I have a saying that says, "being a prophet only works when you agree with God!"

In the prophet lies the secretive treasures of God's heart. It is in the heart and mind of God that his very will resides. This shows the trusted and open relationship between God and his prophet. Satan, known as Lucifer had a very close and trusted relationship with God. He was once the chief musician in heaven with God. Satan became arrogant and entertained a spirit of greed. This greed led him into desiring the space and opportunity to dethrone God and with high hopes take his place. This got Lucifer dethroned from what little authorities God had given him as well as being thrown into a place that was dark, void and empty. I think the more taunting reality of Satan's dethroning was the fact that he was struck down to a place that was beneath his abilities and with no chance of ever being restored. He lost his place in God's kingdom and was replaced by humanity. This is the reason why he hates humanity. More importantly he lost out on having an everlasting and good friendship with God almighty. When Satan sees how man is enabled to do all of the things that he could once do, it infuriates him. Satan can never be saved from the sure fires of the lake of fire nor the torment of hell. However, humans have this chance to be saved and used by God. Satan hates it.

Now that we have laid the foundation of how special prophets and humanity are to God and why the devil hates them so, let's move into what warfare has to do with your prophetic calling. Prophetic warfare has everything to do with an attack on God, his kingdom and everything that he represents. Prophets are carriers of this kingdom of God. They carry the spoken word of the Lord. When God speaks, he intends to fulfill his word. When the prophet enters into warfare It usually happens in 3 phases. These phases are: prophetic receiving, prophetic processing and prophetic fulfillment. Let's look more into these 3-dimensional levels of warfare:

1. Prophetic receiving- When you go up to pray as a believer and especially a prophet of God to hear from him you have got to know that the devil or demonic representatives are going to show up to. Have you ever decided to go pray and on your way to your prayer spot you felt robust (energetic), but when you finally made it to your prayer room all of a

sudden you felt overwhelmingly tired and within 5 minutes of praying you lost interest? Have you ever felt a call to pray in your spirit and then struggled to connect with the spirit of prayer? Have you ever got into your prayer mode and then all of a sudden fell asleep? These are all demonic warfare attacks from the pits of hell. The assignment of this attack is to keep you from making that connection with God in order that you could receive a divine deposit in your spirit. When the prophet prays the secrets of the Lord are released. The enemy does not want you to become a praying prophet because he wants you to remain on the outer courts of where God is. If you ever learn to tap in deeper through God you will become more knowledgeable about the thing/s that are hidden from your prophetic visual. The attack is to keep you with a prophetic title but with no prophetic message. Its job is to keep you with as little prophetic momentum as possible. You can't run with excitement of the things that you do not know. In Job 1:6, it was when the sons of God became purposeful to go up to meet with God that the devil reared his ugly head. Young prophet you have got to know that anywhere Satan shows up that there will be some sort of confusion. Satan is always at war with God's word to impede it from reaching his prophets/people. It is in times when God wants to talk with his prophets to release a word into them that the devil will show up. I encourage you to ask God for inner strength to push through your prayer's young prophet. Receive ye the word of the Lord.

2. Prophetic processing - In this phase of dimensional warfare that the devil shows up to fight you the hardest with holding on to belief of what God said due to what you are

having to fight through. I feel led to remind you again young prophet that the war is NOT against YOU but against what you have in your belly (a word from God). It is in this space of time that you are in between prophecy and fulfillment. This is where the devil will fight you in every aspect of your life. This is the most trying stage of prophetic warfare because you will be tried through people, fought in your mind, emotions, finances and at times in your dream world. The purpose of this stage of attack is to discourage you so to the point where you will give up before making it to prophetic fulfillment. I want to be candid with you that it is in this stage that you will cry the most, feel the heaviest weight, have the hardest prophetic cramps, sweat the most, etc.. It is in this stage that you will have a need to watch what you say so that you do not kill your own fulfilment. This is ultimately the plan of the enemy. However, God will see you through if you only hide in him and refuse to quit.

3. Prophetic fulfillment - Congratulations! You made it to prophetic fulfillment. However, this is surely not the time to drop your hands and become lase. Though you have fought through to make it to fulfillment, you must prepare to fight to stay in fulfillment. In this phase the devil will use people to find ways and reasons for you to become disqualified. This will ensure that you lose what you fight so hard to obtain. It is in this stage that you will need to operate in excellence so that your enemies will not find fault in you but most importantly so that God will find no fault in you. This will be the

phase where you will need to go into deeper consecration so that you do not defeat yourself by becoming guilty of the negative talk that will surely arise against you.

Many people do not make it to phase three because they got defeated in phase one of two. However, there are some that have strapped on the whole armor of God to be able to withstand the wiles of the enemy. Young prophet, the warfare will be great but always remember that according to 1 John 4:4, you have the greater one residing in you and ever ready to become strength to make it to prophetic fulfillment.

Part 27: The Prophet and Holiness

Living holy should be at the top of every prophet's desire. having the integrity and character of God is key to a keen and developed prophetic ministry. To have integrity means to do what is right when no one is watching. It is what you do in your private life. Having character is how you represent God before people. What you do in the dark (privacy) is directly tied to how you will act publicly. It was the words of God to the nation of Israel found in Leviticus 19:2, that came as a challenge to provoke the consciousness of man. This challenge to man was to raise the standard of God in their daily lives. "Be Ye Holy, for I am Holy." This short phrase is filled with the sentiments of God's heart in that men should seek to be like him. Young prophet, there is nothing more that God desires than for you to be like him. In this section we will examine how the Lord desires that the prophet not settle for just the appearance of holiness (image). We will also look at how the Lord is not impressed with our prophetic mantles as much as he is pleased with a life that reflects his holiness.

While sitting at my desk I heard the Lord say, "Many prophets speak truth but their vessels are unclean; however I can use anyone." It was this quote from the Lord when He said, "I can use anyone," that caught my attention. I realized that it was because we are being used that we don't pay close attention to the error of our ways. It's in moments like these that we calculate the validity of the uprightness of our relationship with the Lord.

We base our holiness off of the movement of our gifts. This is dangerous. Let's look at a scripture found in Hebrews 12 :14 (NIV): " Make every effort to live in peace with everyone and to be holy; without holiness no one will see the Lord." This verse shows us that if we live a life without holiness we will not have eternity with God. Another way of looking at this scripture is that if we do not live a holy lifestyle we will not encounter the greater benefit of experiencing God on earth. Our lives will be dry and we will live under a limited window instead of springing forth into the harvest that is associated with "seeing" God.

Holiness is not a denomination but I want you to see how holiness is a lifestyle. It is not what you say only but it is what you "do." Holiness is a title that is given to some religious dignitaries such as the Pope and the Orthodox patriarchs. However, as we look through our news archives, we can clearly see that some, not all, of such dignitaries have not always lived up to such a title. From molesting children, same-sex activities, money laundering, adultery many have failed to exemplify such responsibilites as is tied to "holiness." However, we pray that God will change them. You see, Holiness is not what we wear, how we talk, no make-up, no jewelry, not eating pork or sea animals. Holiness is our upright relationship with the Lord. Holiness is having the ability to hear God about how you should live and then following through with it. Let's look at what the Apostle Paul said in 1 Corinthians 10:23 (NKJV) : "All things are lawful for me, but not all things are helpful; all things are lawful for me, but not all things edify." It is to my understanding that this scripture speaks to the fact that while we may have the liberty to do certain things, it will be to no benefit of you or those who watch your lifestyle. This scripture brings us into the realization that when we are called to holy living, it is not only about us but also about helping to build up the ones that watch you. This takes having the Holy Spirit to fulfill.

The reason why we need God to impute his holiness upon us is because without it we would claim to be his true ambassadors without having the evidence of being such. What this means is that we would:

- Lie

- Cheat

- Steal

- Fornicate

- Commit adultery

- Be lazy

- Rebel against God

While still claiming to be a child of God. Something is wrong with this picture. If the unsaved person is trying change and desires to be saved and they see you sinning as much as they do, it will be hard for you to win them over to Christ. They would see no reason to change. What holiness does is that it puts a distinction between the clean and the unclean. Leviticus 10:10 (KJV) "And that ye may put difference between holy and unholy, and between unclean and clean."

Look at what the Apostle Paul says in Romans 7 :19- 23 (NKJV) : "19 For I do not do the good I want to do, but the evil I do not want to do—this I keep on doing. 20 Now if I do what I do not want to do, it is no longer I who do it, *but it is sin living in me* that does it. 21 So I find this law at work: Although I want to do good, evil is right there with me. 22 For in my inner being I delight in God's law; 23 but I see another law at work in me, waging war against the law of my mind and making me a prisoner of the law of sin at work within me." The message in these verses is that if we do not put the sin in us to death, then we will find ourselves living a double standard by preaching, prophesying and teaching while still embracing fornication, lying etc... This brings on a reproach. Sad to say, but this ungodly behavior reflects the lives of many prophets today. However, God is using this manual to remind you young prophet that you do not have to be counted among them. Let's look at what Jude 24 says : "Now unto him that is able to keep you from falling, and to present you faultless before the presence of his glory with exceeding joy." Some of you may see this section as a little hard. I hear you in my spirit, "Gosh! So you expect us to never fall?" I am not saying that you will not be tempted, but I am saying that you do not have to fall prey to it, thus becoming tainted. Many people feel that because they are being tempted that they are already tainted and should go ahead with the temptation at hand. This is not so. I teach people with this saying, "be tempted, but don't fall." It is Satan's job to tempt us with unholy acts. However, the Holy Spirit can keep you winning by not falling prey to the enemies tactics.

Young prophet you were called by God to raise up the standard of holiness. Never allow anyone to make you feel bad about the Godly life choices that you are making as a youth. I encourage you to keep praying like the prophet Daniel. Keep weeping like the prophet Jeremiah. Keep obeying God while being ignored like the Prophet Ezekiel. Keep allowing God to give you eagle sight like the Prophet Isaiah. Stay humble before the Lord. Don't answer those who mock and scoff at your ministry. Always remember that you are the chosen of the Lord. Keep striving for holiness. Keep going!

Part 28: The Prophet and People

Dealing with people is not easy but it is possible. When you think about people you must think about their personalities. A lot of prophets have a hard time connecting with people. The bulk of this is because they are different. For most prophets they meet people's spirit before meeting them in the flesh. The "thing" that people are trying to conceal at times have already been revealed to the prophet by way of the spirit. This at times can cause the prophet to not have balance while dealing with people. Instead of fully embracing people they will resend based upon what was revealed. I can hear someone ask the question,"well, why would God reveal the secret things to the prophet if they won't receive these people on account of their sinful acts?" This is a good question. When the prophet does not receive a person based upon their issues it's only because they are not mature with seeing the person's "sin" and yet embracing them. In order to help train the prophet for his prophetic calling, God will reveal some harsh things to them and then teach them how not to accept their sin but how to love and embrace the person. In these lessons, God will teach the prophet how to walk out the scripture that says,"by love and kindness have I drawn them."

The prophet will mistakenly shun the person because they have not learned how to balance their emotions about what's been revealed. However, God will usually deal with the prophet in private to ensure them of the assignment that they now have for that person. The prophet will learn to embrace these people while praying for them to be set free. God will also train the prophet to know that not everyone will be their assignment, but that he just wanted them to know who they are dealing with. In situations like this will the prophet need to show love but they will not be subject to carry them in their spirits.

Prophets can be viewed as being weird at times. This is not because they are doing "quirky things", but only because they do not think, act or behave like the average person. When everyone is going left, they feel led to go right. When people are saying, we should turn North, the prophet is that one that will usually stand up and say, "no we should go South." So, they usually rub people the wrong way. I think this is a more enjoyable subject for me to write about because throughout my life I have heard people misrepresent the "loneliness" of a prophet. We touch more on this subject in the lesson, "The Prophet and Seclusion." However, I would like to correct the statement that, "prophets are lonely." While a vast amount of their time is spent alone, they are not lonely. God is ever with them. More so, I want to point out that God made us to be relational and interdependent beings. A part of a human's holistic health involves relationships. It is unhealthy to believe that you can live 50, 60, 70, 80, 90 years etc. on earth without involving other people into your life. While a vast part of your prophetic walk will be alone God will ensure that he provides space for his prophets to have fellowship with other people. I want to tell you that Jesus had friends according to Luke

2:41-44 (NIV). Prophets need people. They need people not only for ministry but also for leisure. I often say that it will take a special person to befriend a prophet. They can be tough to walk with because they can be moody; however, God has people tailor made for them that will understand them and love them genuinely. I am a prophet and I do not have a "best-friend." One thing that I can say is that I am appreciative of the Lord for allowing me to have associates and few friends because it helps to keep me balanced. People are good for the prophet. Due to the prophet spending a majority of his or her time alone, they can get stuck there and will need assistance with transitioning out of this place. In order to help the prophet transition from that alone season with God into having fellowship with others, he will give them a vision. The only way that this vision will be done is if they involve other people. Having relationships with people is healthy for the prophet. Having contact with people will help the prophet be more grounded, resourceful and relatable with the world around them. Young prophet, because of the prophetic assignment that's been entrusted to you, you cannot afford to live in a shell. As a matter of fact, if you struggle with relating with others pray this simple prayer:

"Father in Jesus name, I come to you because I have a need. I am being plagued with the issue of not connecting with my assignment which involves people. Help me Lord to let down my guard and to enjoy humanity so that I may be pleasing to you." God will bring people into the prophets life for various reasons such as:

i. Business relationship

ii. mentor relationship

iii. coach relationship

iv. ministry relationship

v. friendships for leisure

Most prophets are very guarded people. This is typically due to having gone through multiple dysfunctions as it relates to dealing with people. However, God

will heal them if they allow him to in order that they go on to enjoy the people that he has designed for them. Let God in and for our sake let people in.

Part 29: The Prophet and Greed

The love of money is the root of all evil. Notice how the scripture teaches that there is nothing wrong with having money, but how that the problem arises with the love thereof. Sadly, there has been exposure on how some prophets are building ministries with a gain of finances as the root agenda. In this section we will look at how having the love of money can damage you and your ministry. We will also discuss how paying your tithe and giving your offerings and seed sowing will help to keep you and those connected to you under the umbrella of protection and blessings. We will define the different forms of blessings that God will shower down on you as a result of you keeping pure motives of money, having no attachment to money as well as giving when unctioned by the Lord.

Greed can be defined as an overly desirous crave for anything especially for wealth, fame and power. It is an intense selfish desire which only has self in view. This spirit will have you constantly running after possessions, attention, money, positions, preaching engagements, honor, etc... Danielle Bernock from the article, "what is Greed? Definition and Bible verses about Greed," says that "Greed is a spiritual disease of the heart affecting all areas of a person's life." It is my theological perspective that greed can be either godly or ungodly. It is godly according to Matthew 4:2; Luke 4:2 and ungodly according to 1 Timothy 6:10. This spirit of greed has plagued people to the point where many have taken other people's lives. This spirit of greed is usually the wicked force behind 2 other spirits according to proverbs 1:19:

1. robbery and

2. murder

Prophets need to stay free from this spirit of greed. Let's examine how this spirit of greed can influence the spirit of the prophet of God. Remember now, while the prophetic call or mantle is pure in the beginning, the vessel can become impure and devious when influenced by an unclean spirit such as the spirit of greed.

1. When the prophet entertains greed, he is overly zealous and pious to have something in his possession that he does not have. If the prophet is not careful, he will intentionally try to impede or hinder the next man's elevation. This would be done with hopes that he will take that person's place. This spirit of greed will use the prophetic vessel to rob a person of their blessings.

2. Another spirit that could escalate from the spirit of greed is a murderous spirit. This spirit's motive is to kill off anything that has what its desire is. It feels threatened by any person that has what it wants so it would seek to murder you either psychically or spiritually to ensure that it gets what you have. Let's look at how this looks:

a. seeking to speak negatively into the ear of those that want to favor someone with the thing that it desires.

b. seeking to kill the perspective of a person that's not as strong in order to make them not desire the thing that is their inheritance. In doing this will it ensure the person with this spirit of greed that they will inherit it instead of the one that it was meant for.

c. literally murdering someone over something they have

3. The funny aspect about this spirit is that it's not that the person with this spirit of greed does not have possessions of their own. This spirit just makes a person unsatisfied with what they already have. So, we can see that lack is not always the motive behind greed as much as it is feelings of dissatisfaction.

Let's look at what I meant in that there could be a "godly" greed. In the article, "what is Greed? Definition and Bible verses about Greed," Danielle Bernock wrote that the term Greed comes from the old English word "graeding," which means "always hungry for more." The Holy Spirit took me to Matthew 4:2 as well as Luke 4:2 on how in both book accounts it reads, "Jesus afterward hungered." If you look a little deeper into a more spiritual aspect this verse was talking about how Jesus had entered an insatiable place. Jesus was already on a 40 day and night fast while being tempted by the devil. When you go on a fast you usually encounter the deeper things of God, so Jesus was probably on an all-time spiritual high. When you talk about an insatiable place it's not that you haven't already experienced something, but it's that after your experience you know somewhere in your spirit that there is more to encounter with God. If we look at Luke's account in chapter 4 it records how that the devil left him for a more opportune time. This meant that this devil that was fighting Jesus was only leaving him for a short time and was coming again to tempt him once more. Jesus knew that if he was to gain the total victory over the devil that he had a need to stay in a spirit of greed where he would hunger after God all the more. It is in times where we are hungry after God that we are more spiritually fortified to handle the wiles of the devil. In my belief this is the only time that prophets can become greedy in that they are heavily seeking after God. I'm sure God won't take offense.

Galatians 5:23- walking in the fruit of the spirit against there is no law

Part 30: The Prophetic Mind

In this section we will talk about the prophet and his mind. Possessing the mind of Christ is simply having the thoughts of Christ. Philippians 2:5 (KJV) "Let this mind be in you, which was also in Christ Jesus." The prophetic mind is an advantage for the church. Having the prophetic mind gives the prophet the ability to lead from the future. The prophet that has the prophetic mind causes the church to be one step ahead of the church. This causes the church to not have to wait until something happens in order to get ready; we get ready in advance. Dealing with the prophet's mind is about servitude towards God and people.

Having a prophetic mind is confidence in God yet lowliness of thought/heart/spirit as in submission. Philippians 2:6 (NIV), " Who, being in very nature God, did not consider equality with God something to be used to his own advantage." The mind of Christ is filled with humility. Having this kind of mind moves you into high dimensional thinking. The person that has the mind of Christ is given the ability to ascend into the heavens to gain the heavenly perspective of God.

What does a prophetic mind do?

Having the mind of Christ is all about the exaltation of God. In order to do this, one would have to be willing to abandon all of their rights that they may fulfil the agenda of God. Let's look at Philippians 2:7-8 (NLT), "Instead, he gave up his divine privileges; he took the humble position of a slave and was born as a human being. When he appeared in human form he humbled himself in obedience to God and died a criminal's death on a cross." Jesus knew of the plan as to why God sent him to the earth. This purpose was for him to die in order that mankind would have the opportunity to be regenerated and to live with God for eternity. This is what having a prophetic mind does for the prophet in that it causes him or her to have a willing heart to abandon their personal agenda and to adopt God's agenda for their lives. Most times when a prophet is in the beginning stages of his or her prophetic call they have plans for their ministry. Most times the plans that they have and what God intends for them do not match. It will take having a humble spirit to be able to let go and to fully embrace what God says. When the young prophet is told that they will be "great," most times they immediately think about traveling throughout nations, preaching before large crowds, living large, etc.. While this may be the case for a few it certainly is not the fate of many prophets. When the angel of the Lord told John the Baptist father that he would be great in the sight of the Lord, it was because of what John's prophetic assignment was in his era. What would make John ``great" in God's eyes would be because he would turn many of the Israelites to the Lord. Let's look at Luke 1:15-16 (BSB), " for he will be great in the sight of the Lord. He shall never take wine or strong drink, and he will be filled with the Holy Spirit even from his mother's womb. 16 Many of the sons of Israel he will turn back to the Lord their God." Yes crowds were drawn to John the Baptists' ministry meetings. However, the crowds would come because

John would baptize them with water, preach the good news, and point them towards God (the source of their help). John exemplified what a true prophet of God does which is to point people to Christ. They realize that it is not about them.

Another portion of having a prophetic mind means that God will establish the right train of thoughts in your mind to ensure that you are walking towards your prophetic fulfillment. It is almost impossible for you as a prophet to walk out your prophetic assignment without having the mindset to match where you are going. To help the prophet not walk in a state of confusion, God will elevate their mind where he or she should be in order to keep them relevant.

Those with a prophetic mind also esteem others higher than themselves. It is scriptural to do so. Let's look at Philippians 2:3 (KJV), "Let nothing be done through strife or vainglory; but in lowliness of mind let each esteem other better than themselves." Prophets are called and chosen by God. This is because God has people in mind that he would like to reach through their prophetic ministry. Though the prophet is given access into the mind, authority and power of God, he must not think that he will be effective with using such privileges without people. The prophet is called to serve both God and man. This is why he must embrace humility.

We have learned that having a prophetic mind is all about submission towards God and humility towards people. It always leads the prophet down the road of telling God "yes" concerning the will of God for his or her life. I admonish you prophets to ask God to give you a prophetic mind.

Part 31: The Prophet and Word Practicality

Preaching has its place. However, it is not good enough for the prophet to preach as much as it is for him to practice what he preaches. If we look at the life of Jesus, the prophets of old and the Disciples of that era, they all held a secret to their ministries. This secret was the demonstration of the message of the kingdom of God in which they all preached. These men were different from the Pharisees, Sadducees, Essenes and Zealots. It was the manifestation of the kingdom of God in their lives and through their lives that brought true change to their followers. This is where we are now. The Lord dropped in my spirit in that these are the last days and the last generation. What people are looking for is not in word only but also in deeds. Jesus is looking for people who will "ACT" on the word so that men may see just how glorious his power is. He wants to use "YOU", young prophet to show forth the excellency of his might. The greatest validity to your prophetic ministry will be that you preach on subjects that you have lived out. For you young prophet, there will be a greater and more effective approach in your ministry when you look like what's coming out of your mouth. In this will you challenge your listeners to rise to the standard of the word of God.

Faith is an action. It is impossible to say that you have faith without movement upon the word you recieve. Hebrews 4:2 (NIV), " For we also have had the good news proclaimed to us, just as they did; but the message they heard was of no value to them, because they did not share the faith of those who obeyed." Words without mobility will leave you with high hope, yet without manifestation. The word mixed without faith profits you nothing. Your faith is the practicality of words which will always point to movement. You cannot have faith without movement. Once again, it is the practice of the word. Every action is associated with proof. God has given us the scroll (Word of God), in order that we might know how to conduct our lives. Practicing the word will move one in the direction of evidence. I feel led to prophesy here, that God wants to give you evidence in your prophetic ministry. People may try to deny that you are God's chosen prophet. When they see the evidence of your prophetic words come alive, blind eyes opening, dumb spirits rebuked, etc.. as a result of your prophetic mantle and authority; they will no longer have grounds to disbelieve.

For every word that God speaks there is fruit attached. There is a blessing for one to receive according to the word spoken to them. Let's examine what Mary said when the angel of the Lord came to her with a decree from heaven's throne. It was said that she would be overshadowed by the power of the Holy Spirit and conceive a son which she should call Jesus: Luke 1:38 (NIV),"I am the Lord's servant, Mary answered. May your word to me be fulfilled." Then the angel left her." Another part of the word from the angel was for Mary to go visit Elizabeth. Mary did not only call herself blessed after receiving a word from the angel, but she also obeyed the other part of the instruction by "going." Mary was able to have an earthly witness to the spoken word over her life because she confessed that it could happen for her, believed and went. Let's look at what Elizabeth said in Luke 1:45, "Blessed is she who believed for there will be a fulfillment of those things which were told her from the Lord." When the Lord speaks a word into your life, it is because he intends to bring forth fulfillment in your life. Like with Mary moving out upon the word of the Lord, we need movement upon the spoken word of God so that we can see what God said manifest in our lives for his glory. Amen!

We have been called and anointed to represent God well. He wants us to move upon his word with integrity and character. David said, "thy word have I hidden in thy heart so that I might not sin against thee." It is the will of God that we elevate in him by receiving, preaching and acting on the word. It is his will that we do not have a form of godliness. It is his will that we have a demonstration. The power of any word lies within your practice.

Part 32: Displaced Prophets

The Lord reminded me on how I should write in this section. There are times when if not careful the prophet can become displaced. This simply means that They are in a region that does not match their spherical authority. In this section, we will discuss how each prophet is given an assigned region to which his or her prophetic abilities will become most effective. When within his or her prophetic zone, there is an easier flow and level of access granted the prophet. It is when the prophet steps outside of the perimeters placed by God, that he or she will step onto war zones not developed or chosen to fight. The prophet will undergo great rejection from the residents of the land, encounter unusual demonic attacks, struggle and walk under closed heavens. When displaced, the Lord will find no pleasure in you and he will bring you to a place of decision to get back into place.

To be displaced means to be out of alignment with truth. According to Merriam Webster displaced means to have the place of; to replace. However, it is my strongest belief coming from a more spiritual viewpoint that to be displaced means to be out or range or out of touch with one's domain. In the prophet's sense, to be out of range with one's prophetic sphere, authority and power. For the prophet this can be deadly. Prophets are designed to thrive under certain prophetic atmospheric regions. The greatest efforts of their prophetic beings and ministry is directly connected to the places where God has sent and established them. Any work they do outside of these prophetic perimeters will not count towards their prophetic assignments in the earth. (Read Matthew 7:22)

There are so many prophets who are just doing works as a means to make themselves feel significant. They fail to realize that when they are dedicated to the place and work that God has put them, they will always have significance. For the prophet, it's never about the "doings" of works as much as it is about their obedience to the prophetic works that God has asked them to do. The production of fruit is what God holds in highest regard. The prophet needs to not be concerned about the quantity as much as the quality of their works. Young prophets do not get into the mindset of thinking that the more works you do the more valuable you are. For the prophet, God can give you 3 major assignments throughout the span of your prophetic reign and these 3 assignments can have the effect on hundreds, thousands and even millions of people.

So many prophets have been displaced by senior voices. Some prophets have allowed space for the counsel of man, more so than a listening ear for the counsel of God. In the kingdom of God today, we have prophets who were born prophets but are in positions that do not match their prophetic destiny. As a result, many are frustrated and are spiritually dying. The spiritual attack from the devil to keep you from operating in your prophetic place is to keep you from tapping into strength in order that you spring forth into your prophetic livelihood. On the contrary, there are prophets that have heard their prophetic assignments but like Gideon downplayed who they are. These are not displaced by men but by their own folly. They downplay who they are and the assignment that God has given them in order not offend the people around them. This is why as a prophet of God you need only to walk with people who have been given a revelation of who you are as a prophet by God. If this does not happen you will find yourself always dummying down your prophetic rank and thus miss out on the life that God has planned for you prophetically.

Prophets have got to be assured in their spirit that they are already accepted in the beloved. They must hear God strongly about what they are supposed to be doing as well as the location that they are supposed to be doing so. They must feel comfortable in their own skin as well as in their place in the kingdom of God. The prophet must never allow themselves or others to displace them out of the prophetic place that they have been chosen by God to operate from. Let's examine some ways that being in your prophetic place can help you and your ministry:

1. Springs forth spiritual health

2. Your effectiveness reaches beyond barriers

3. You and those who are submitted under your prophetic voice flourishes

4. You attract wealth and favor for your prophetic assignment

Let's examine what happens when you abandon your true prophetic calling:

1. Your full potential is blocked

2. You become limited in revelatory access

3. You become stagnated

4. You will become a frustrated prophet

Let's look at what happen with the young prophet who started out right but ended up a displaced prophet 1 Kings 13:

☐ Most displaced prophets start out on the right track but at times end up displaced at the word of "senior prophetic voices." This could be due to the prophet's desire to be accepted by those with whom they feel are like them (prophetic). As prophets there is a need to feel as though you belong somewhere and to be in a place where you can let your guards down and just "be". Young prophet though you honor those who are senior to you, you must also always try the spirit by the spirit. It is a must that you know the spirit of those with whom you interact.

Part 33: The Prophet and Focus

In this section we will discuss how you will find that after you have decided to stay in your place, your focus will become more defined and your thoughts clearer. We will discuss how to stay free from distractions, how to keep your mind free from junk email and how to be content with what's been placed in your prophetic view. While there is much going on and great competition, young prophet the body of Christ will gain more from you when you decide to mind your business and stay in your lane.

Focused people almost always obtain most of their goals in life if not all of them. To be focused means to be goal-oriented and determined to fulfill it. In order to be focused you have to have vision before you. The prophet must become sure of the direction that he or she God is steering them towards. He must develop a mindset that is in compliance with the journey he must take towards fulfillment. As I am sitting here at my desk, I see a picture of an old testament prophet in my head. This prophet is on the floor rocking back and forth in communication with God while receiving prophetic vision for his life. I can see this prophet rising up and is now walking forward with great confidence because he now had a focal point. I can hear the Lord saying that this is what focus does for the prophet in that it gives him or her surety of his purpose in the earth.

Let's examine some of the things that usually disrupts the prophet:

1. It is my opinion that the number one thing that disrupts the prophets focus is usually lack of prayer. For any believer the lack of prayer is the blind fold upon their eyes. This is especially true for the prophet. When you lose connection with the visionary (God), you lose your focal point which is your vision.

2. The second thing that disrupts the prophets focus is the lack of study. To have vision with no study of the vision you will surely lose focus. Study is like guidance to the prophet's prophetic eye and sensitivity on how to move towards the manifestation of their vision. 2 Timothy 2:15 is a key verse that every prophet should cling to. While the Apostle Paul was talking to the church of Ephesus to study God's law, it is my belief that the prophet or average Christian should study the bible along with other resourceful book, magazine, blog, newspaper, article etc. materials. Ultimately every prophetic vision extenuates from God's word. The Apostle Paul encourages us to study the word which is the prophetic blue-print for every personal and corporate vision from God.

3. The third thing that can distract the prophet is not writing the vision down. It was the prophet Habakkuk that wrote in 2:2 how we should write the vision down. The purpose for this is so that people could study it in order that they might be empowered to run with the vision. This is because they have a focal point. Writing down the vision is vital because it can help the prophet to not become competitive and out of apostolic alignment with the visions of others that will surround him or her.

4. The fourth thing that disrupts prophetic focus is having too many voices in your ear. Stop! Take a deep breath because we are going to spend a moment on this distraction. Let me begin with myself by saying that I do not believe in having too many voices in my ear gate. I am over 30 years old now and while under the leadership of 3 churches throughout my life span, I have never sought the mentorship or leadership or other voices. I have always believed that If God sent me to be a part of these churches then what I needed spiritually was in the leader of that church. This is not to say that I would reject the word of the Lord from other leaders, but that I have never felt the need to go behind my leaders back to gain counsel from other people. God has always provided me with a prophetic and sufficient leader who had a voice of instruction and direction for my life. I have engaged in conversations with few where it seemed as though they made it their lifelong goal to have more than one voice in their ear gate. What a tragedy. This was only a tragedy only because these people's motives were not all pure. While listening to these Indvidual's speak, I would discern that the only reason they were seeking other voices was on account of causing confusion with their leader. They would seek to sit in the presence of these people to glean insight only to take it back to their leaders and gloat in their presence what some other leaders was counseling them on. However, I have seen how it backfired in that instead of the leader becoming jealous and confused, the individual would wrestle with a spirit of confusion only because they did not know that the voices that they were seeking were manipulating voices with an agenda.

5. The fifth thing that can distract the prophet from focus is dealing with consistent warfare and not knowing how to choose their battles. Sometimes one of the prerequisites of being a prophet is to be warfare-savvy. During seasons when warfare is heavy the prophet can get distracted by the fight and lose focus of the promise. Ultimately the devil sends warfare to detour the prophet from pressing towards their prophetic promise. dealing with hindrances, setbacks, delays etc. can cause the prophet to shift their focus and cause a mental drain. Once the prophet enters into mental drain, he or she will not have the strength to carry on in the vision at hand. It's a strategic plan from Satan. This is why it's good for the prophet to have a strong support system where he or she could receive a boost in their spirit when needed. Young prophet, it's ok to admit that you are in need of a boost. It's ok to call someone who knows you is genuine towards you to help pray you through.

6. The sixth thing that distracts the prophet is having to deal with people. Please understand my heart in that not all people are a disgrace to be around. There are some people that being around them makes life a little easier to endure. The way they can make you laugh, how they serve in needed capacities, how they are sensitive to you spiritually, etc. all makes being a part of the human race a blessing. However, young prophet because you are gifted and pure some people will draw near to you to drain you and to taint your spirit. People can have a tendency to draw near to the prophet to drop a lot of: "news" into their ears for the purpose of gaining their trust. Some people will come to agitate the

prophet's spirit. They will do and say things intentionally just to bring your spirit low. I encourage you to discern the hearts and ask God to reveal the motives of people so that you will know how to best handle them.

Part 34: Prophets and the Holy Spirit

In the Old Testament, we could see how the Holy Spirit moved among or upon the prophets. In the New Testament we can clearly see how after the death of Jesus Christ, this same Holy Spirit was now given permission to enter into the prophets in order that they might move prophetically. Rather, the Holy Spirit moved upon the prophet or was operating from within the prophet, we can see that it was an important factor for the prophet and Holy Spirit to have a strong connection. It is said that the prophet gives direction. The Holy Spirit knows the way. He is the wind which blows. In this section we will examine that because prophets of God are called to be forerunners for Christ, they will need the assistance of the Holy spirit to do so. John the Baptist is a perfect example

There was a promise that the father had spoken through Jesus to the apostles in that they would receive the Holy Spirit. However, according to acts 1:4 this promise would be given on two accounts:

1. They stay in Jerusalem

2. They wait

The treasure in their waiting was that it gave them access to God's power. Read what Acts 1:8 (NKJV). The other part of Acts 1:8 reveals or unveils what man's assignment would be while receiving this power. Let's further read what the scripture says, "and you shall be witnesses to me in Jerusalem, and in all Judea and Samaria, and to the end of the earth." Do you see what I see? I'm glad you do. Yes! This means that you have work to do. I can hear someone saying, "uh-oh! Maybe I should not have received him (holy spirit) so soon. :) When you receive the Holy Spirit, you become empowered to not only read, have knowledge and look wonderfully important. No, it's your help to be led during your spiritual Journey. It is because your prophetic assignment is spiritual that you will need the assistance of the Holy spirit which governs the spirit world to accompany you. You cannot do your prophetic assignment without the Holy Spirit. Let's look at Acts 1:2, He through". Most often prophets that sit in the office of the prophet are called to be a leader in some capacity in the Lords Kingdom. This means that God will give them a team at some point in their prophetic journey that they will need the Holy Spirit's guidance to help them lead.

So, we can see so far how that the Holy spirit is the wind that carries one through their journey. Without having it is like the blind leading the blind. Having the Holy Spirit gives you the ability to see and hear God for clear instructions. Let's look at some examples of how prophets were led by the Holy spirit:

i. John the Baptist- "And he will turn many of the sons of Israel to the Lord their God, and he will go before him in the spirit and power of Elijah, to turn the hearts of the fathers to the children, and the disobedient to the wisdom of the just, to make ready for the Lord a people prepared." (Luke 1:16–17)

ii. Ezekiel- "God grabbed me. God's Spirit took me up and sat me down in the middle of an open plain strewn with bones. He led me around and among them - a lot of bones! There were bones all over the plain - dry bones, bleached by the sun. He said to me, "Son of man, can these bones live? I said, "Master God, only you know that. " He said to me, "Prophesy over these bones: Dry bones, listen to the Message of God!" (Ezekiel 37:1-4)

iii. Prophets- "For prophecy never had its origin in the human will, but prophets, though human, spoke from God as they were carried along by the Holy Spirit." (2 Peter 1:21)

Let's look at some ways that the Holy Spirit can come upon you?

i. Ezekiel 2:2-spoken over

ii. Matthew 10:1- breathed upon

iii. Acts 1:4- tarrying attracts the Holy Spirit

Part 35: The Prophet and Rest

"Rest young prophet! Rest!" I want to combat the lie that others have taught you or that you have thought that resting makes you lazy or that it can cause you to become a quitter. Being lazy and resting are two different actions. When you are lazy, it simply means that you lack the necessary interest and actions needed to be fruitful. It means that you are ok with settling with less than what your potential can produce. However, when you rest, it simply means that you retreat from the "norm" in order to refocus, refresh and re-align your vision concerning your prophetic assignment. I grew up in an Apostolic house where our Apostles, prophets, evangelists, pastors, teachers and lay members took sabbaticals. The Apostolic leadership encouraged everyone to rest. They understood that rest was one of the major tactics to combat burn-out. People who are burned out end up quitting.

Hebrews 4:9-10 says, "And there shall remain a rest for the people of God. For he who has entered his rest has himself also ceased from his works as God did from his." Rest is simply freedom from disrupted peace. The Hebrew word for rest is "Nuach." This means to be quiet. Sometimes this word nuach is used synonymously with the word shabat, which means to cease or to rest. (biblehub.com) The Greek word for rest is "anapausis" meaning cessation or refreshment. (biblehub.com) Being a prophet of God can be very demanding. The scripture says to whom much is given, much is required. When you are called to walk in the office of the prophet you will have a dual assignment. The first assignment is to minister to God. The second assignment is to minister to the people. This means that you will have the weight to serve both God and man. What a demand. God has high needs and so do people. However, the Lord will give you the prophetic capacity to handle the weight of your assignments. The scripture found in 1 Corinthians 10:13, brings comfort in that God will not put more on you than you can bare. People will try to and you will put more demands on yourself, but you will need to monitor this and not feel pressured to take on assignments out of your strength or tolerant range. If not careful the prophet will become so overwhelmed by the demands until he or she will become agitated, easily frustrated and distracted away from what is most important. Another danger of not taking rest from your prophetic assignment, is that you will continue on doing your work but on a low performance level. This is another tactic that the devil will use against you. He has no problem with you being in your prophetic assignment just as long as you are too tired, distracted and frustrated to perform at your highest potential.

Let's examine what psychologist says are signs of fatigue:

1. High irritability level

2. Paranoia sets in

3. Lack of focus

4. Loss of appetite

The scripture teaches us that even Jesus in all his supremacy found it necessary to include solitude time in his daily life. Jesus was a man full of power and compassion. He knew that the fame of his name had gone out and when people would see him, they would bombard him with all of their issues, problems and requests. Jesus knew of the demands of his day and wisdom spoke out to him and led him into quiet places. It was in these quiet places that Jesus found refreshment for the journey ahead of him.

Let's look at some scriptures on rest: (READ)

1. Matthew 11:29-30

2. Mark 4:39

3. Isaiah 48: 22

4. Jeremiah 31:25

5. 1 Chronicles 22:9

Part 36: The Prophet and Rejection

Like a rectangle unfit for a circle and a fish unfit in the tundra biome, so is the prophet unfit for the systems of this world. We are in this world but we are not of this world. This means that the habitat that we live out of is not of this Babylonian cosmos but of a heavenly domain. Only those that live out of the heavenly realm will be able to identify with others that live there as well. The people that live in this world and are of this world will most likely reject those who live in the heavenlies with God. This is because there is enmity between God and the devil and because they will not understand the people that do not operate as they do.

For the prophet, rejection is like another license gained as a sign of approval for such ministry. Rejection can be defined as one unacceptance as being a part of any institution, group, organization, etc. This rejection can really be to the prophet's advantage because they won't have the pressure of "keeping" up with others. They will be at liberty to set standards, start trends and to become the kind of approved leader that God has intended for them to be come. If the prophet does not learn to see rejection as his advantage, it will become his disadvantage in that he could easily succumb to having a fear of man and never "become" his true self. He will live limited and will never thrive into his greatest potential if he does not learn to properly handle rejection.

Disadvantages of rejection:

If not careful the prophet will develop some if not all of the following issues:

1. Suicidal war zones

2. Depression

3. No social/limited social life (bad for brain activity-could cause dementia and Alzheimer's)

4. Health issues- weight gain, dangerous weight loss, loss of appetite, organ and tissue damage

5. Live under blockages-bound up spiritually

6. Entertain a spirit of bad fear

7. Poor self-perspective and low self-value

8. Live his life hiding. He will live under the lie that in order to keep himself from hurt, he must hide away from the human race

Advantages of Rejection:

For the prophet, rejection is inevitable. Either of himself or his gift will experience an all-time high of rejection. However, if he gains the right interpretation of this rejection it could or out for his good:

1. Rejection can be a perfect time for the prophet to draw closer to God

2. In a noisy world that constantly crave for your attention, you will gain the delightful season of limited or no distractions

3. When you are rejected you can discover your true self because no one is in your ear telling you who they think that you are

4. Purpose and direction for your life is defined more

5. Your prophetic senses will become more keen

6. You will develop a stronger confidence in God and yourself

7. Your focus will become more astute

What does the bible say about rejection?

Let's examine how some of the prophets dealt with rejection. Let's begin with what Jesus said about the prophets: "a prophet is without honor except in his own house (Luke 4:24). 2 Chronicles 18:6-7 ; 14 (Micaiah)- because he was hated and rejected by the king of Israel and his house, Micaiah was willing to lie in order to please the king and be accepted. The Apostle Paul underwent rejection by the hands of his contemporaries found in Philippians 1, yet he was faithful with preaching the gospel of Jesus Christ.

Jesus and Rejection at the hands of men

Jesus was rejected at Nazareth Luke 9:53; 4:16-30) This rejection was on account of Jesus knowing who he was and because he was able to break free out of the box that people created for him, they sought to kill him.

Rejection from God

- Cain (Genesis 4:3;5) Cain disrespected God in his giving and the Lord in return rejected him and his offering. As a result of this rejection from the Lord did Cain entertain a spirit of anger and his countenance had fallen. Cain was so angry that he refused to have dialogue with God to confess his anger and féeling of rejection out of pride. This led him to plot against his brother and eventually murder him later.

- Sarah (Genesis 16:2-3) Sarah felt rejected by the Lord because he had not opened her womb so that she could bear Abram a child. As a result of her desperation she had given her maid-servant Hagar to Abram to sleep with her and produce her a child. She was willing to take a plan that was not given by the Lord and accept it as his perfect will.

- Saul (1 Samuel 15:10-11;26; 28:6-7) Saul got rejected by the Lord due to his own folly of lying to the prophet about his obedience to the Lord. He had only done partially what the Lord required of him and testified that he had fully obeyed the

Lord. Saul did not know that his sins would find him out in the noisy bleating of a calf. As a result of God's rejection, Saul turned to mediums.

- Woman rejected by the Lord when she went to seek help from Jesus due to her daughter's sickness. Though she was turned away and likened unto the dogs she continued to pursue until she received what she needed from God.

We can see that rejection happens to everyone. However, though you feel the pain when in the middle of it you must decide that it will not move you outside of the will of God.

Part 37: The Prophet and Suffering

It is my opinion that in the fivefold ministry it is the prophet and the Apostle which identifies the most with a facet of Jesus' life and ministry that no other ministry gift relates. This side of Jesus that the prophets are most acquainted with is Jesus' suffering. Please do not misunderstand me with thinking that I am disregarding the truth that all ministry gifts suffer for Christ's sake. However, the kind of suffering that the prophet goes through is to help them to know what it was like to be Christ and to feel what he went through in order that the prophet would be most humble.

Why does God choose suffering as a tool to humble the prophet?

I remember years ago when the Lord told me that the walk and life of a prophet was a "continual" death. I thought surely, I can die but once (lol). As I got older the Lord helped me to understand what he meant in that the walk in the prophetic arena was a daily death to one's self and to the things of this world. The spirit of pride is a very big battle for the Lord's prophets. Many of the Lord's prophets are conceited, arrogant and battle with self-entitlement. Many walk with the mentality that people owe them something. Prophets are special and are taught that they are special. The bible refers to them as being great. However, many take this and pervert it because they feel as if everything should be handed to them on a silver platter. Many fail to realize that to whom much is given much is required. In order for God to use them mightily he has to take the prophet through a breaking and a bruising. This could take a short time or a long time depending on how cooperative the prophet is. If the prophet is not broken or does not go through suffering, he or she will not have a great compassion as Christ did for the people. Another point to suffering is that Jesus suffered at the hands of people and it pleased the lord. However, this caused Jesus to turn his attention towards God with fasting and prayer. This suffering taught him how to call on Abba father. It was through his suffering that he learned the beauty of obedience. This is true for the prophet as well in that he will learn to obey God more so than man when he has suffered a while.

What is normally birth out of the prophets suffering?

1 Peter 5:10, ESV: "And after you have suffered a little while, the God of all grace, who has called you to his eternal glory in Christ, will himself;

- Restore

- Confirm

- Strengthen

- Establish you

All Apostles are prophets but not all Prophets are Apostles. So, with saying this let's examine the Apostle Paul and his suffering. Let's see what was produced from his suffering. 2 Corinthians 12:9-10- It seems as though God granted the Apostle access to his power through his sufferings. This suffering looked like:

1. Infirmities

2. Reproaches

3. Having needs

4. Persecutions

5. Distresses

Notice the "es" on all these types of suffering. This means that there are many levels to these types of sufferings. To the level that you suffer will be the level of power you operate out of. Each level of suffering carries the reward of power to the one that endures until the end.

Does the Prophet suffer throughout his or her life or is it just temporary?

I'm reminded of the late brother Brilla. We loved Brother Brilla. He would come to our service to expedite our choir anniversary programs. There was one song that he would always sing. This song was entitled: "My Soul is anchored in the Lord" by the late Reverend Douglas Miller. The part that comes to mind is when he sings, "I've had some good days. I've had some hills to climb. All of my good days outweigh my bad days and I won't complain. The meaning to these words is to say that there are seasons of suffering as well as seasons of relief. However, this will happen for as long as we live on this earth.

God will be with you through it all.

Part 38: The Prophet and Leadership Ability

When God called the prophet to service it was always for him to become a voice; a leading voice. God infused his message into the prophet in order that he would use him to go be a leader to the people that God would send him too. Most often, the prophets that God chooses are those who do not desire leadership capacity. These prophets carry the ability to lead yet they would rather be the christian without any responsibility for other people. This is why God wants to use them in leadership roles. They will not rise up to take Gods' glory.

Prophets are chosen to be in the front. This at times can take decades before the prophet accepts his call. I think this delay could be accounted to the fact that they may not know exactly what area they are called to lead. This will take time. However, the prophet has got to just start moving in his call. The deeper he goes into his prophetic calling, he will begin to know his prophetic leadership roles. Most times God will give the prophet a passion for the area of leadership that he or she is called to lead. Sometimes the prophet will embrace the passion of the particular area but reject the leadership role that comes with it. This could cause the prophet to settle with receiving only a portion of his purpose and never walking in the full potential of who he was called to be.

Lack of confidence to lead can be a potential reason as to why the prophet will not rise in leadership. Another cause could be the fear of being attacked. Being a leader is more mental than anything. John the Baptist was coming to bring revival to man's mind in order that he would be free from the hindrances that would arise. When you can see attacks through the lens of maturity, it will cause you to handle them better and will cause you to maintain your composure. I did not want to take a leadership role because I did not like dealing with people all of the time. I would not mind dealing with them for a short while but I like alone time and I did not want all of my time taken away. God has and is still training me to not be selfish. I now have private sessions with people at least 4 days out of my week. I must say that I enjoy speaking with them. This is accounted to God helping me and because we discuss topics that I feel prepared to talk about. So I say, get ready, young prophet. Read a book a month. Stay current with today's world. Pray and ask God to equip you to lead his people. You can do it. If I can. I know you can.

I say you are bold. You are courageous. You are capable. You can do all things through Christ because he will give you strength. You are a leader. Rise up and take your place.

Part 39: Prophetic Authorities

What exactly is prophetic authority? According to Oxford Languages, authority is the power or right to give orders, make decisions, and enforce obedience. This means that you have supremacy and jurisdiction from the Lord and have been given a measure of rule. Prophetic authority is an authority based on grace and favor, not position. This is possible because you can have a position with no authority. Someone of supreme authority has to give you the right and sanction to operate with such duties.

1. **Prophets have Priestly anointing:**

   - Ezekiel- Ezekiel 1:3 (NIV), "the word of the LORD came to Ezekiel the priest, the son of Buzi, by the Kebar River in the land of the Babylonians. There the hand of the LORD was on him."

2. **Prophets have Kingly anointing:**

   - Jesus Christ- 1 Timothy 6:14-15 (ESV), " to keep the commandment unstained and free from reproach until the appearing of our Lord Jesus Christ, which he will display that the proper time he who is the blessed and only Sovereign, the King of kings and Lord of lords...,"

   - David- 2 Samuel 5:1-4 (NIV), " All the tribes of Israel came to David at Hebron and said, "We are your own flesh and blood. In the past, while Saul was king over us, you were the one who led Israel on their military campaigns. And the Lord said to you, 'You will shepherd my people Israel, and you will become their ruler.' "When all the elders of Israel had come to King David at Hebron, the king made a covenant with them at Hebron before the Lord, and they anointed David king over Israel. David was thirty years old when he became king, and he reigned forty years. In Hebron he reigned over Judah seven years and six months, and in Jerusalem he reigned over all Israel and Judah thirty-three years." Acts 2:29-30 (BSB), "Brothers, I can tell you with confidence that the patriarch David died and was buried, and his tomb is with us to this day. But he was a prophet and knew that God had promised him on oath that He would place one of his descendants on his throne."

3. **Authority to send forth a prophetic message:**

- 2 Kings 5:10-14 (NIV), "Elisha (Prophet) sent a messenger to say to him, "Go, wash yourself seven times in the Jordan, and your flesh will be restored and you will be cleansed." But Naaman went away angry and said, "I thought that he would surely come out to me and stand and call on the name of the Lord his God, wave his hand over the spot and cure me of my leprosy. Are not Abana and Pharpar, the rivers of Damascus, better than all the waters of Israel? Couldn't I wash in them and be cleansed?" So he turned and went off in a rage. Naaman's servants went to him and said, "My father, if the prophet had told you to do some great thing, would you not have done it? How much more, then, when he tells you, 'Wash and be cleansed'!" So he went down and dipped himself in the Jordan seven times, as the man of God had told him, and his flesh was restored and became clean like that of a young boy."

4. **Authority to anoint those appointed to leadership:**

- 1 Samuel 16:13 (NIV), "So Samuel took the horn of oil and anointed him in the presence of his brothers, and from that day on the Spirit of the Lord came powerfully upon David. Samuel then went to Ramah."

- Deuteronomy 34:9 (NIV), "Now Joshua son of Nun was filled with the spirit of wisdom because Moses had laid his hands on him. So the Israelites listened to him and did what the Lord had commanded Moses."

5. **Authority to build schools to train other prophets:**

- 1 Samuel 19:18-22 (CEV), "Meanwhile, David went to Samuel at Ramah and told him what Saul had done. Then Samuel and David went to Prophets Village and stayed there. Someone told Saul, "David is at Prophets Village in Ramah." Saul sent a few soldiers to bring David back. They went to Ramah and found Samuel in charge of a group of prophets who were all prophesying. Then the Spirit of God took control of the soldiers and they started prophesying too" When Saul heard what had happened, he sent another group of soldiers, but they prophesied the same way. He sent a third group of soldiers, but the same thing happened to them. Finally, Saul left for Ramah himself. He went as far as the deep pit at the town of Secu, and he asked, "Where are Samuel and David?" "At Prophets Village in Ramah," the people answered."

6. **Authority to cast out demons (illegal abode in vessels):**

- Mark 9:38-40 (NIV), "Teacher," said John, "we saw someone driving out demons in your name and we told him to stop, because he was not one of us. Do not stop him," Jesus said. "For no one who does a miracle in my name can in the next moment say anything bad about me, 40 for whoever is not against us is for us."

- 1 Samuel 16:23 (CEV), "Whenever the evil spirit from God bothered Saul, David would play his harp. Saul would relax and feel better, and the evil spirit would go away."

7. **Authority to shift regions through intercessory prayer:**

   - Read the entire chapter of Daniel 9 in the Contemporary english version (CEV)

   - Read 1 Samuel 2: 1-10 in the Contemporary English version (CEV.) You will find the prophetic prayer of Prophetess Hannah.

8. **Authority to lead nations:**

   - Joseph- Genesis 41:41 (NLT), "Pharaoh said to Joseph, "I hereby put you in charge of the entire land of Egypt.""

   - Moses- Exodus 3:11 (NLT), "But Moses protested to God, "Who am I to appear before Pharaoh? Who am I to lead the people of Israel out of Egypt?""

   - Samuel- 1 Samuel 3:20 (NIV), "And all Israel from Dan to Beersheba recognized that Samuel was attested as a prophet of the Lord." 1 Samuel 7:15-16 (NIV), " Samuel continued as Israel's leader all the days of his life. From year to year he went on a circuit from Bethel to Gilgal to Mizpah, judging Israel in all those places."

9. **Authority to direct/instruct all people:**

- Common men- 2 Kings 4:1-7, "The wife of a man from the company of the prophets cried out to Elisha, "Your servant my husband is dead, and you know that he revered the LORD. But now his creditor is coming to take my two boys as his slaves." Elisha replied to her, "How can I help you? Tell me, what do you have in your house?" "Your servant has nothing there at all," she said, "except a small jar of olive oil." Elisha said, "Go around and ask all your neighbors for empty jars. Don't ask for just a few. Then go inside and shut the door behind you and your sons. Pour oil into all the jars, and as each is filled, put it to one side." She left him and shut the door behind her and her sons. They brought the jars to her and she kept pouring. When all the jars were full, she said to her son, "Bring me another one." But he replied, "There is not a jar left." Then the oil stopped flowing. She went and told the man of God, and he said, "Go, sell the oil and pay your debts. You and your sons can live on what is left.""

- Elite men- 1 Samuel 10:8 (NIV), "Go down ahead of me to Gilgal. I will surely come down to you to sacrifice burnt offerings and fellowship offerings, but you must wait seven days until I come to you and tell you what you are to do." (The Prophet Samuel is instructing King Saul.)

10. **Authority to unfold the prophetic plans of God for mankind:**

- Genesis 49: 1-28 (NIV), "Then Jacob called for his sons and said: "Gather around so I can tell you what will happen to you in days to come. "Assemble and listen, sons of Jacob; listen to your father Israel. "Reuben, you are my firstborn, my might, the first sign of my strength, excelling in honor, excelling in power. Turbulent as the waters, you will no longer excel, for you went up onto your father's bed, onto my couch and defiled it. "Simeon and Levi are brothers— their swords are weapons of violence. Let me not enter their council, let me not join their assembly, for they have killed men in their anger and hamstrung oxen as they pleased. Cursed be their anger, so fierce, and their fury, so cruel! I will scatter them in Jacob and disperse them in Israel. "Judah, your brothers will praise you; your hand will be on the neck of your enemies; your father's sons will bow down to you. You are a lion's cub, Judah; you return from the prey, my son. Like a lion he crouches and lies down, like a lioness—who dares to rouse him? The scepter will not depart from Judah, nor the ruler's staff from between his feet,until he to whom it belongs shall come and the obedience of the nations shall be his. He will tether his donkey to a vine, his colt to the choicest branch; he will wash his garments in wine, his robes in the blood of grapes. His eyes will be darker than wine, his teeth whiter than milk. "Zebulun will live by the seashore and become a haven for ships; his border will extend toward Sidon. "Issachar is a rawboned donkey lying down among the sheep pens. When he sees how good is his resting place and how pleasant is his land, he will bend his shoulder to the burden and submit to forced labor. "Dan will provide justice for his people as one of the tribes of Israel. Dan will be a snake by the roadside, a viper along the path, that bites the horse's heels so that its rider tumbles backward. "I look for your deliverance, LORD. "Gad will be attacked by a band of raiders, but he will attack them at their heels. "Asher's food will be rich; he will provide delicacies fit for a king. "Naphtali is a doe set free that bears beautiful fawns. "Joseph is a fruitful vine, a fruitful vine near a spring, whose branches climb over a wall. With bitterness archers attacked him; they shot at him with hostility. But his bow remained steady, his strong arms stayed limber, because of the hand of the Mighty One of Jacob, because of the Shepherd, the Rock of Israel, because of your father's God, who helps you, because of the Almighty, who blesses you with blessings of the skies above, blessings of the deep springs below, blessings of the breast and womb. Your father's blessings are greater than the blessings of the ancient mountains, than the bounty of the age-old hills. Let all these rest on the head of Joseph, on the brow of the prince among his brothers. "Benjamin is a ravenous wolf; in the morning he devours the prey, in the evening he divides the plunder." All these are the twelve tribes of Israel, and this is what their father said to them when he blessed them, giving each the blessing appropriate to him."

- 1 Samuel 9:15-17 (NIV), "Now the day before Saul came, the LORD had revealed this to Samuel: "About this time tomorrow I will send you a man from the land of Benjamin. Anoint him ruler over my people Israel; he will deliver them from the hand of the Philistines. I have looked on my people, for their cry has reached me." When Samuel caught sight of Saul, the LORD said to him, "This is the man I spoke to you about; he will govern my people.""

Young Prophet you are the chosen of the Lord. While you have to grow in your prophetic anointing you will also have to wait on God to measure the level of authority that comes with your prophetic territory. Do not allow anyone to give you an authority that God has not approved for you to walk in. Authority in the hands of the immature or unprepared can cause damage to your prophetic ministry. Wait on God.

Part 40: Methodologies of God

Every prophet is unique. While being raised in an Apostolic House, The Leader taught us how that God works with both the personality and learning styles of each individual. We all learn in different ways and so God will communicate with us as such. There are many ways that God communicates with his Prophets. The typical methods of how God speaks to His prophets are as followed:

- **Visions:**

    Definition- visual perception; ability to see something (Dictionary.com)

    Scriptural Example- Acts 18:9-10 (NIV), "One night the Lord spoke to Paul in a vision: "Do not be afraid; keep on speaking, do not be silent. For I am with you, and no one is going to attack and harm you, because I have many people in this city.""

- **Dreams:**

    Definition- a series of thoughts, images, and sensations occurring in a person's mind during sleep (Dictionary.com)

    Scriptural Example- Genesis 28:10-15 (NIV), "Jacob left Beersheba and set out for Harran. When he reached a certain place, he stopped for the night because the sun had set. Taking one of the stones there, he put it under his head and lay down to sleep. He had a dream in which he saw a stairway resting on the earth, with its top reaching to heaven, and the angels of God were ascending and descending on it. There above it stood the Lord, and he said: "I am the Lord, the God of your father Abraham and the God of Isaac. I will give you and your descendants the land on which you are lying. Your descendants will be like the dust of the earth, and you will spread out to the west and to the east, to the north and to the south. All peoples on earth will be blessed through you and your offspring. I am with you and will watch over you wherever you go, and I will bring you back to this land. I will not leave you   until   I   have   done   what   I   have   promised   you."

- **Face to face:**

  Definition- people involved being close together and looking directly at each other. (Dictionary.com)

  Scriptural Example- Exodus 33:11 (NIV), "The LORD would speak to Moses face to face, as one speaks to a friend. Then Moses would return to the camp, but his young aide Joshua son of Nun did not leave the tent."

- **Audibly:**

  Definition- hearing ability

Scriptural Example- Ezekiel 1:3, "The word of the Lord came expressly unto Ezekiel the priest, the son of Buzi, in the land of the Chaldeans by the river Chebar; and the hand of the Lord was there upon him." Ezekiel 12:25, "For I am the LORD: I will speak, and the word that I shall speak shall come to pass; it shall be no more prolonged: for in your days, O rebellious house, will I say the word, and will perform it, saith the Lord GOD."

- **Through angels:**

  Definition- a spiritual being believed to act as an attendant, agent, or messenger of God. (Dictionary.com)

  Scriptural Example- Luke 1:11-13, "And an angel of the Lord appeared to him, standing to the right of the altar of incense. Zacharias was troubled when he saw the angel, and fear gripped him. But the angel said to him, "Do not be afraid, Zacharias, for your petition has been heard, and your wife Elizabeth will bear you a son, and you will give him the name John."

- **Scripture:**

  Definition- Word of God

  Scriptural Example- Matthew 6:11, "Give us this day our daily bread." (this bread is the word of God. Daily he desires to speak with us through scripture.)

- **Imagery:**

   Definition- visually descriptive or figurative language, especially in a literary work. (Dictionary.com)

   Scriptural Example- Acts 7:30-31, "After forty years had passed, an angel appeared to Moses in the flames of a burning bush in the desert near Mount Sinai. "When Moses saw it, he marveled at the sight; and as he approached to look more closely, there came the voice of the Lord..."

- **People:**

   Definition- Human beings

   Scriptural Example- 1 Peter 4:11 (KJV), "If anyone speaks, let him speak as the oracles of God." 1 Corinthians 12:8 (KJV), "for to one is given the word of wisdom through the Spirit, to another the word of knowledge through the same Spirit,.."

- **Mind/thoughts:**

   Definition- brain, intelligence; a person's mental process. (Dictionary.com)

   Scriptural Example- Colossians 3:2 (NIV), "Set your minds on things that are above, not on things that are on earth." (This is because with the prophetic mind God is descending his word from an upward position and not downward position; therefore the prophet should keep his mind on things above and not lowly   matters.)

- **Elements:**

Definition- nature

Scriptural Example- Joshua 10:12 (ESV) , "At that time Joshua spoke to the LORD in the day when the LORD gave the Amorites over to the sons of Israel, and he said in the sight of Israel, "Sun, stand still at Gibeon, and moon, in the Valley of Aijalon." Psalms 19:1 proclaims, "The heavens declare the glory of God; and the firmament shows His handiwork." 2 Samuel 22:14, "The LORD thundered from heaven, And the most High uttered his voice." 1 Kings 19:12, "And after the earthquake a fire; but the Lord was not in the fire: and after the fire a still small voice."

- **Signs:**

Definition- a gesture or action used to convey information or instructions. (Dictionary.com)

Scriptural Example- Isaiah 7:14, "Therefore the Lord Himself will give you a sign: Behold, a virgin will be with child and bear a son, and she will call His name Immanuel."

We can see how God will use a variety of ways to communicate with his prophets. Communication is key to any relationship. The prophet will need to be open to all methods of how God speaks. This will ensure that the prophet does not become familiar with God and miss the opportunity to receive a message when he is desirous to reveal his secrets to them. I was counseling with someone who has a prophetic mantle on their lives. In the middle of our conversation they interrupted me to ask me if I would help them identify the way God speaks to them. This was a heavy question because surely no one should know when God is speaking to them but them. However, by the help of the Lord I answered with this question, "How well do you learn?" The individual was able to help tell me. I then said to them that that probably would be the way that God would choose to communicate with them the most. However, I also told them not to box God in. God has a way of changing his methodology of communication. This could be because he is awakening another part of who you are as a prophet and it could be that he is now ready to reveal to you another part of who he is and how he operates. In the dialogue with God there lies his secrets. Young prophet I encourage you to not get caught up with the "hows," until you miss the "what's." Just be open. Allow God to choose the way he speaks with you. Enjoy his secrets as he unfolds his heart to you.

Part 41: Prophetic Pain

1 Peter 4:14 (NIV), "If you are insulted because of the name of Christ, you are blessed, for the Spirit of glory and of God rests on you." Young prophet when you're called to the prophetic ministry, do not expect to be loved and embraced by everyone. Infact, the people that you will expect to be the most excited for your ministry assignments will be the very ones fighting you both publicly and privately. typically with the prophetic ministry, it is the outcasts that will likely be drawn the most to your ministry. This will be because they will feel that you understand what its like to be them and will embrace them as they are. This is very true. So in essence, the ones that you think will support your ministry will not and the ones you would not expect to support you, will. I once heard a preacher say, "it's less pain felt when you are open for it instead of being in denial and closed off from it." This brings me to making my point with Joseph. I think because Joseph was so young and innocent that he would never in a million years think that his own family would reject him and his dream. I mean if you couldn't tell anyone, you would at least have hopes of expressing your dreams with your close family and friends. This was not the case with Joseph. This young boy was put to sleep by God and given a dream by God. When he got up from the dream he found out the hard way that he would not be celebrated for it, but that he would be plotted against. What a tragedy.

Genesis 37:2, "This is the account of Jacob's family line. Joseph, a young man of seventeen, was tending the flocks with his brothers, the sons of Bilhah and the sons of Zilpah, his father's wives, and he brought their father a bad report about them." We can see here that Joseph did not give a bad report about all of the brothers but only the sons of Bilhah and Zilpah which were: Dan, Naphtali, Gad and Asher. This is significant. We will see why later.

Genesis 37: 3, "Now Israel loved Joseph more than any of his other sons, because he had been born to him in his old age; and he made an ornate robe for him." In this verse we can see how the true love of Israel is being expressed through his gift of a coat to Joseph. Notice how that the scriptures never mention how that Israel did not love the other sons, but only that he loved Joseph more.

Genesis 37: 4, "When his brothers saw that their father loved him more than any of them, they hated him and could not speak a kind word to him." I learned that the underlying reason for this hatred from his brothers was not on account of the dream or that he was loved by his father. The underlying reason for Joseph being hated by his brothers was on account of their knowledge of the father's love for Joseph. Sometimes people will inflict pain on you not on account of what they don't see but on account of what they can see. The bible says that it was when the other brothers "saw" this love that Israel had for Joseph that they hated him. Some people don't mind you being loved just as long as it's never expressed to you in a way that they can see it. Sad to say young prophet, but there will be some people who will hate to see you being blessed. However, it will be your maturity level and perspective that will determine how well you handle this level of pain.

Genesis 37:5, "Joseph had a dream, and when he told it to his brothers, they hated him all the more." We can see that Joseph's dream only intensified the hate that was already in their hearts towards him. Sometimes God will give you a dream that will only provoke the true feelings of people towards you. This will help you early on to know who and who not to walk with.

Lets track where this prophetic pain could have possibly started with Joseph. Genesis 37:23, "So when Joseph came to his brothers, they stripped him of his robe, the ornate robe he was wearing and they took him and threw him into the cistern. The cistern was empty; there was no water in it.:" This is where I believe Joseph was infused with greater pain. There he was on his way to see if everything was well with his brothers only to have them seek to take his life. Another point that I want to make is that they thought that stripping Joseph of his coat would be good enough to destroy his dream. They fail to realize that while the coat was given by his natural father, his dream was given by the almighty father. Anything that the almighty father gives cannot be destroyed by death threats. Like Joseph, God will keep you alive so that the dream will speak forth and not die.

Young prophet I want to encourage you that just as Joseph had encountered pain at the inception of his journey as a prophet, you too might encounter pain. Though Joseph carried this pain all throughout his ministry, God had brought him to a place where he could release it. You would have thought that he would have released all of his anger while in prison but he did not. Lets look at a verse in Genesis 43:30, "Deeply moved at the sight of his brother, Joseph hurried out and looked for a place to weep. He went into his private room and wept there." Genesis 50: 17-18, "Joseph wept when they spake unto him." And his brethren also went and fell down before his face; and they said, Behold, we be thy servants." It was not until Joseph was faced again with the people that caused him this pain, that he wept. However, Joseph was able to weep a little better because by this time he was in a greater position in the earth as ruler and relationally with God. In Genesis 50:18, we can also see how Joseph was able to witness what God showed him as a young boy come to pass with his brothers bowing before him.

Sometimes, while on this prophetic journey it will seem as if God has forgotten about us. Joseph's life looked nothing like what he saw in that dream when he started his journey. He went through many long and painful seasons. Some in which he probably felt was of no purpose. I'm sure there were seasons where he wanted to die. Young prophet, I submit to you that just as Joseph was able to make it to the fulfillment of what God said without dying or giving up, so will you. Like Joseph, God will provide a place of healing for you. You will wept one day. You will look up and find yourself standing in the promises of

God. Your pain may seem forever but it won't be forever. Don't quit because your pain has purpose.

Bonus: The Joy of being a Chosen Prophet of the Lord

I chose to write about the joys of being a prophet of the Lord last because I wanted you to be encouraged to know that even after rejection, suffering, warfare, seclusion, etc... that there is hope in the end. While all of what we discussed in these books can seem overwhelming, you must know that there is light at the end of the tunnel. God will cause there to be great sunshine where there was darkness. You must know young prophet that the greater the gory in your life the greater the glory. Yes, there shall be glory after this. Jesus was getting ready to go through his storms and hard trials yet he endured because he had a prophetic outlook of what the end was going to be. Hebrews 12:2,

"[looking away from all that will distract us and] focusing our eyes on Jesus, who is the Author and Perfecter of faith [the first incentive for our belief and the One who brings our faith to maturity], who for the joy [of accomplishing the goal] set before Him endured the cross, disregarding the shame, and sat down at the right hand of the throne of God [revealing His deity, His authority, and the completion of His work]."

Young prophets don't give up when things get rough. be like Jesus with knowing that there is joy and a reward on the other side of your pain. Like Jeremiah you may be called to preach to people who are willing to kill you. Like Ezekiel, you may be called to prophesy to a rebellious house. Like Daniel, you may be plotted against on account of your prophetic stance. With all of the evil that was plotted against these prophets of the

Lord, we can clearly see how that the Lord did not allow any of them to be harmed beyond bearable conditions and neither were they killed before their time. When you are called to live in a certain era because God wants to use you, you will not die before your time on account of foolishness.

Know that with pain and suffering also comes the great joy of seeing people get delivered, saved and set free as a result of your persistence. Do not fold up while going through a season of great pressure and persecution. You will go through seasons of being unsupported and will have to keep encouraged through self-talk. There will be other seasons when you will have the support of man. However, always remember that as a prophet not to depend on man for validation. Some of you will never know what it's like to have thousands of followers; and we say to God be the glory. Some of you God will allow for you to have lots of followers; and we say to God be the glory. There is one follower that you should always be looking for and that is Jesus Christ. As long as he is there to cheer you on you will be in good standing.

Know that you will not rise to fame because you think you should or because you are doing all of the 'perks.' The prophetic ministry is different. God will raise you up due to the fact that he has deposited a word in your belly to speak forth with great clarity and precision. You don't get to control the thermostat of your ministry; God does. When God opens the door everyone will witness the confirming word that flows through you. Be encouraged by the young prophet. You have a great work ahead of you. I celebrate you. Whenever, you feel discouraged just turn to this page and read here where it says, "Prophetess Ashley believes in and celebrates you!" God bless you on your journey. I love you but God loves you most!

https://www.ashleyreynoldsministry.com/

www.ingramcontent.com/pod-product-compliance
Lightning Source LLC
Chambersburg PA
CBHW081139090426

42736CB00018B/3415